# Welcome Insiders!

If you're reading this then you have taken the first steps in controlling your finances. After all, your money should not tell you what to do! This simple planner will help you keep money where it belongs...in your bank account!

*-Brittany Dobbins*

# PLAN IT!
## What's Your Purpose?

## What are your short-term financial goals?

## What are your long-term financial goals?

# THE BUDGET
## Know your income and expenses

### Income

PAYCHECK #1      $_____

PAYCHECK #2      $_____

PAYCHECK#3      $_____

TOTAL      $_____

### Expenses

HOUSING

| CREDITOR | DUE DATE | MO. PAYMENT |
|----------|----------|-------------|
| _____ | _____ | _____ |
| _____ | _____ | _____ |
| _____ | _____ | _____ |
| _____ | _____ | _____ |
| _____ | _____ | _____ |
| _____ | _____ | _____ |

# THE BUDGET
*Know your income and expenses*

## LOANS/DEBT

| CREDITOR | DUE DATE | MO. PAYMENT |
|----------|----------|-------------|
|          |          |             |
|          |          |             |
|          |          |             |
|          |          |             |
|          |          |             |
|          |          |             |

## UTILITIES

| CREDITOR | DUE DATE | MO. PAYMENT |
|----------|----------|-------------|
|          |          |             |
|          |          |             |
|          |          |             |
|          |          |             |
|          |          |             |

# THE BUDGET
*Know your income and expenses*

## INSURANCE

| PROVIDER | DUE DATE | MO. PAYMENT |
|----------|----------|-------------|
|          |          |             |
|          |          |             |
|          |          |             |
|          |          |             |
|          |          |             |
|          |          |             |

## SAVINGS / INVESTMENTS

| PROVIDER | DUE DATE | MO. PAYMENT |
|----------|----------|-------------|
|          |          |             |
|          |          |             |
|          |          |             |
|          |          |             |
|          |          |             |

# THE BUDGET
*Know your income and expenses*

## Expenses

## MISC. EXPENSES   [GYM MEMBERSHIPS ETC.]

| PROVIDER | DUE DATE | MO. PAYMENT |
|----------|----------|-------------|
| _____ | _____ | _____ |
| _____ | _____ | _____ |
| _____ | _____ | _____ |
| _____ | _____ | _____ |
| _____ | _____ | _____ |
| _____ | _____ | _____ |

TOTAL EXPENSES          $_____

# CREDIT CARD TRACKER
*Knowing your limits*

| PROVIDER | DUE DATE | MO. PAYMENT |
|----------|----------|-------------|
| _____ | _____ | _____ |
| _____ | _____ | _____ |
| _____ | _____ | _____ |
| _____ | _____ | _____ |
| _____ | _____ | _____ |
| _____ | _____ | _____ |

TOTAL INCOME     $_____

− TOTAL EXPENSES     $_____

= TOTAL EXPENSES     $_____

# THE REVIEW
## How did you do this month?

_____

_____

_____

_____

_____

_____

_____

_____

_____

_____

_____

_____

_____

# Accountability Check!

Did you stick to your goals? Is your budget on track or did you have a moment of weakness? Was retail therapy part of your budget this month?

# THE BUDGET
## Know your income and expenses

## Income

PAYCHECK #1     $_____

PAYCHECK #2     $_____

PAYCHECK#3     $_____

TOTAL     $_____

## Expenses

### HOUSING

| CREDITOR | DUE DATE | MO. PAYMENT |
|----------|----------|-------------|
| _____ | _____ | _____ |
| _____ | _____ | _____ |
| _____ | _____ | _____ |
| _____ | _____ | _____ |
| _____ | _____ | _____ |
| _____ | _____ | _____ |

# THE BUDGET
## Know your income and expenses

## Expenses

### LOANS/DEBT

| CREDITOR | DUE DATE | MO. PAYMENT |
|----------|----------|-------------|
| _____ | _____ | _____ |
| _____ | _____ | _____ |
| _____ | _____ | _____ |
| _____ | _____ | _____ |
| _____ | _____ | _____ |
| _____ | _____ | _____ |

### UTILITIES

| CREDITOR | DUE DATE | MO. PAYMENT |
|----------|----------|-------------|
| _____ | _____ | _____ |
| _____ | _____ | _____ |
| _____ | _____ | _____ |
| _____ | _____ | _____ |
| _____ | _____ | _____ |

# THE BUDGET
## Know your income and expenses

## Expenses

### INSURANCE

| PROVIDER | DUE DATE | MO. PAYMENT |
|----------|----------|-------------|
| _____ | _____ | _____ |
| _____ | _____ | _____ |
| _____ | _____ | _____ |
| _____ | _____ | _____ |
| _____ | _____ | _____ |
| _____ | _____ | _____ |

### SAVINGS / INVESTMENTS

| PROVIDER | DUE DATE | MO. PAYMENT |
|----------|----------|-------------|
| _____ | _____ | _____ |
| _____ | _____ | _____ |
| _____ | _____ | _____ |
| _____ | _____ | _____ |
| _____ | _____ | _____ |

# THE BUDGET
*Know your income and expenses*

## Expenses

### MISC. EXPENSES     [GYM MEMBERSHIPS ETC.]

| PROVIDER | DUE DATE | MO. PAYMENT |
|----------|----------|-------------|
| _____ | _____ | _____ |
| _____ | _____ | _____ |
| _____ | _____ | _____ |
| _____ | _____ | _____ |
| _____ | _____ | _____ |
| _____ | _____ | _____ |

TOTAL EXPENSES          $_____

# CREDIT CARD TRACKER
*knowing your limits*

| PROVIDER | DUE DATE | MO. PAYMENT |
|----------|----------|-------------|
| _____ | _____ | _____ |
| _____ | _____ | _____ |
| _____ | _____ | _____ |
| _____ | _____ | _____ |
| _____ | _____ | _____ |
| _____ | _____ | _____ |

TOTAL INCOME      $_____

– TOTAL EXPENSES      $_____

= TOTAL EXPENSES      $_____

# THE REVIEW
## How did you do this month?

_____

_____

_____

_____

_____

_____

_____

_____

_____

_____

_____

# Money Mantra:

*Financial success is*

# MINE

*I accept it now*

# THE BUDGET
*Know your income and expenses*

## Income

PAYCHECK #1          $_____

PAYCHECK #2          $_____

PAYCHECK#3           $_____

TOTAL                $_____

## Expenses

### HOUSING

| CREDITOR | DUE DATE | MO. PAYMENT |
|----------|----------|-------------|
| _____ | _____ | _____ |
| _____ | _____ | _____ |
| _____ | _____ | _____ |
| _____ | _____ | _____ |
| _____ | _____ | _____ |
| _____ | _____ | _____ |

# THE BUDGET
*Know your income and expenses*

## Expenses

### LOANS/DEBT

| CREDITOR | DUE DATE | MO. PAYMENT |
|----------|----------|-------------|
| _____ | _____ | _____ |
| _____ | _____ | _____ |
| _____ | _____ | _____ |
| _____ | _____ | _____ |
| _____ | _____ | _____ |
| _____ | _____ | _____ |

### UTILITIES

| CREDITOR | DUE DATE | MO. PAYMENT |
|----------|----------|-------------|
| _____ | _____ | _____ |
| _____ | _____ | _____ |
| _____ | _____ | _____ |
| _____ | _____ | _____ |
| _____ | _____ | _____ |

# THE BUDGET
*Know your income and expenses*

## INSURANCE

| PROVIDER | DUE DATE | MO. PAYMENT |
|----------|----------|-------------|
| _____ | _____ | _____ |
| _____ | _____ | _____ |
| _____ | _____ | _____ |
| _____ | _____ | _____ |
| _____ | _____ | _____ |

## SAVINGS / INVESTMENTS

| PROVIDER | DUE DATE | MO. PAYMENT |
|----------|----------|-------------|
| _____ | _____ | _____ |
| _____ | _____ | _____ |
| _____ | _____ | _____ |
| _____ | _____ | _____ |
| _____ | _____ | _____ |

# THE BUDGET
*Know your income and expenses*

## MISC. EXPENSES     [GYM MEMBERSHIPS ETC.]

| PROVIDER | DUE DATE | MO. PAYMENT |
|----------|----------|-------------|
| _____ | _____ | _____ |
| _____ | _____ | _____ |
| _____ | _____ | _____ |
| _____ | _____ | _____ |
| _____ | _____ | _____ |
| _____ | _____ | _____ |

TOTAL EXPENSES          $_____

# CREDIT CARD TRACKER
*Knowing your limits*

| PROVIDER | DUE DATE | MO. PAYMENT |
|----------|----------|-------------|
| _____ | _____ | _____ |
| _____ | _____ | _____ |
| _____ | _____ | _____ |
| _____ | _____ | _____ |
| _____ | _____ | _____ |

TOTAL INCOME          - $_____
TOTAL EXPENSES          $_____
                      = 
TOTAL EXPENSES          $_____

# THE REVIEW
## How did you do this month?

# Accountability Check!

Did you stick to your goals? Is your budget on track or did you have a moment of weakness?

# THE BUDGET
## Know your income and expenses

## Income ● ●

PAYCHECK #1 $_____
PAYCHECK #2 $_____
PAYCHECK #3 $_____

TOTAL $_____

## Expenses ● ●

### HOUSING

| CREDITOR | DUE DATE | MO. PAYMENT |
|----------|----------|-------------|
| _____ | _____ | _____ |
| _____ | _____ | _____ |
| _____ | _____ | _____ |
| _____ | _____ | _____ |
| _____ | _____ | _____ |
| _____ | _____ | _____ |

# THE BUDGET
*Know your income and expenses*

## Expenses

### LOANS/DEBT

| CREDITOR | DUE DATE | MO. PAYMENT |
|----------|----------|-------------|
| _____ | _____ | _____ |
| _____ | _____ | _____ |
| _____ | _____ | _____ |
| _____ | _____ | _____ |
| _____ | _____ | _____ |
| _____ | _____ | _____ |

### UTILITIES

| CREDITOR | DUE DATE | MO. PAYMENT |
|----------|----------|-------------|
| _____ | _____ | _____ |
| _____ | _____ | _____ |
| _____ | _____ | _____ |
| _____ | _____ | _____ |
| _____ | _____ | _____ |

# THE BUDGET
## Know your income and expenses

## Expenses

### INSURANCE

| PROVIDER | DUE DATE | MO. PAYMENT |
|----------|----------|-------------|
|          |          |             |
|          |          |             |
|          |          |             |
|          |          |             |
|          |          |             |
|          |          |             |

### SAVINGS / INVESTMENTS

| PROVIDER | DUE DATE | MO. PAYMENT |
|----------|----------|-------------|
|          |          |             |
|          |          |             |
|          |          |             |
|          |          |             |
|          |          |             |

# THE BUDGET
## Know your income and expenses

## Expenses

### MISC. EXPENSES    [GYM MEMBERSHIPS ETC.]

| PROVIDER | DUE DATE | MO. PAYMENT |
|----------|----------|-------------|
| _____ | _____ | _____ |
| _____ | _____ | _____ |
| _____ | _____ | _____ |
| _____ | _____ | _____ |
| _____ | _____ | _____ |
| _____ | _____ | _____ |

TOTAL EXPENSES          $_____

# CREDIT CARD TRACKER
*Knowing your limits*

| PROVIDER | DUE DATE | MO. PAYMENT |
|----------|----------|-------------|
| _____ | _____ | _____ |
| _____ | _____ | _____ |
| _____ | _____ | _____ |
| _____ | _____ | _____ |
| _____ | _____ | _____ |
| _____ | _____ | _____ |

TOTAL INCOME    - $_____

TOTAL EXPENSES    - $_____

= 

TOTAL EXPENSES    $_____

# THE REVIEW
## How did you do this month?

# Money Mantra:

*My attitude towards*

# MONEY

*is positive*

# THE BUDGET
*Know your income and expenses*

## Income

PAYCHECK #1          $_____

PAYCHECK #2          $_____

PAYCHECK#3           $_____

TOTAL                $_____

## Expenses

HOUSING

| CREDITOR | DUE DATE | MO. PAYMENT |
|----------|----------|-------------|
| _____ | _____ | _____ |
| _____ | _____ | _____ |
| _____ | _____ | _____ |
| _____ | _____ | _____ |
| _____ | _____ | _____ |
| _____ | _____ | _____ |

# THE BUDGET
## Know your income and expenses

## LOANS/DEBT

| CREDITOR | DUE DATE | MO. PAYMENT |
|----------|----------|-------------|
| _____ | _____ | _____ |
| _____ | _____ | _____ |
| _____ | _____ | _____ |
| _____ | _____ | _____ |
| _____ | _____ | _____ |
| _____ | _____ | _____ |

## UTILITIES

| CREDITOR | DUE DATE | MO. PAYMENT |
|----------|----------|-------------|
| _____ | _____ | _____ |
| _____ | _____ | _____ |
| _____ | _____ | _____ |
| _____ | _____ | _____ |
| _____ | _____ | _____ |

# THE BUDGET
## Know your income and expenses

## INSURANCE

| PROVIDER | DUE DATE | MO. PAYMENT |
|----------|----------|-------------|
| _____ | _____ | _____ |
| _____ | _____ | _____ |
| _____ | _____ | _____ |
| _____ | _____ | _____ |
| _____ | _____ | _____ |
| _____ | _____ | _____ |

## SAVINGS / INVESTMENTS

| PROVIDER | DUE DATE | MO. PAYMENT |
|----------|----------|-------------|
| _____ | _____ | _____ |
| _____ | _____ | _____ |
| _____ | _____ | _____ |
| _____ | _____ | _____ |
| _____ | _____ | _____ |

# THE BUDGET
*Know your income and expenses*

## MISC. EXPENSES    [GYM MEMBERSHIPS ETC.]

| PROVIDER | DUE DATE | MO. PAYMENT |
|---|---|---|
| _____ | _____ | _____ |
| _____ | _____ | _____ |
| _____ | _____ | _____ |
| _____ | _____ | _____ |
| _____ | _____ | _____ |
| _____ | _____ | _____ |

## TOTAL EXPENSES         $_____

# CREDIT CARD TRACKER
## Knowing your limits

| PROVIDER | DUE DATE | MO. PAYMENT |
|----------|----------|-------------|
| _____ | _____ | _____ |
| _____ | _____ | _____ |
| _____ | _____ | _____ |
| _____ | _____ | _____ |
| _____ | _____ | _____ |
| _____ | _____ | _____ |

TOTAL INCOME    - $_____

TOTAL EXPENSES    - $_____

= 

TOTAL EXPENSES    $_____

# The Review
## How did you do this month?

---

# Accountability Check!

Did you stick to your goals? Is your budget on track or did you have a moment of weakness?

# THE BUDGET
## *Know your income and expenses*

## Income

PAYCHECK #1          $_____

PAYCHECK #2          $_____

PAYCHECK#3          $_____

   TOTAL          $_____

## Expenses

### HOUSING

| CREDITOR | DUE DATE | MO. PAYMENT |
|---|---|---|
| _____ | _____ | _____ |
| _____ | _____ | _____ |
| _____ | _____ | _____ |
| _____ | _____ | _____ |
| _____ | _____ | _____ |
| _____ | _____ | _____ |

# THE BUDGET
*Know your income and expenses*

## LOANS/DEBT

| CREDITOR | DUE DATE | MO. PAYMENT |
|----------|----------|-------------|
| _____ | _____ | _____ |
| _____ | _____ | _____ |
| _____ | _____ | _____ |
| _____ | _____ | _____ |
| _____ | _____ | _____ |
| _____ | _____ | _____ |

## UTILITIES

| CREDITOR | DUE DATE | MO. PAYMENT |
|----------|----------|-------------|
| _____ | _____ | _____ |
| _____ | _____ | _____ |
| _____ | _____ | _____ |
| _____ | _____ | _____ |
| _____ | _____ | _____ |

# THE BUDGET
## Know your income and expenses

## Expenses

### INSURANCE

| PROVIDER | DUE DATE | MO. PAYMENT |
|----------|----------|-------------|
| _____ | _____ | _____ |
| _____ | _____ | _____ |
| _____ | _____ | _____ |
| _____ | _____ | _____ |
| _____ | _____ | _____ |
| _____ | _____ | _____ |

### SAVINGS / INVESTMENTS

| PROVIDER | DUE DATE | MO. PAYMENT |
|----------|----------|-------------|
| _____ | _____ | _____ |
| _____ | _____ | _____ |
| _____ | _____ | _____ |
| _____ | _____ | _____ |
| _____ | _____ | _____ |

# THE BUDGET
*Know your income and expenses*

## MISC. EXPENSES     [GYM MEMBERSHIPS ETC.]

| PROVIDER | DUE DATE | MO. PAYMENT |
|----------|----------|-------------|
| _____ | _____ | _____ |
| _____ | _____ | _____ |
| _____ | _____ | _____ |
| _____ | _____ | _____ |
| _____ | _____ | _____ |
| _____ | _____ | _____ |

## TOTAL EXPENSES     $_____

# CREDIT CARD TRACKER
*Knowing your limits*

| PROVIDER | DUE DATE | MO. PAYMENT |
|----------|----------|-------------|
| _____ | _____ | _____ |
| _____ | _____ | _____ |
| _____ | _____ | _____ |
| _____ | _____ | _____ |
| _____ | _____ | _____ |
| _____ | _____ | _____ |

TOTAL INCOME     –   $_____

TOTAL EXPENSES    $_____

=   

TOTAL EXPENSES    $_____

# THE REVIEW
## How did you do this month?

_____

_____

_____

_____

_____

_____

_____

_____

_____

_____

_____

_____

_____

# Money Mantra:

*I am*

# A WEALTH

*magnet*

# THE BUDGET
## Know your income and expenses

## Income

PAYCHECK #1          $_____

PAYCHECK #2          $_____

PAYCHECK#3           $_____

TOTAL                $_____

## Expenses

### HOUSING

| CREDITOR | DUE DATE | MO. PAYMENT |
|---|---|---|
| _____ | _____ | _____ |
| _____ | _____ | _____ |
| _____ | _____ | _____ |
| _____ | _____ | _____ |
| _____ | _____ | _____ |
| _____ | _____ | _____ |

# THE BUDGET
*Know your income and expenses*

## Expenses

## LOANS/DEBT

| CREDITOR | DUE DATE | MO. PAYMENT |
|----------|----------|-------------|
| | | |
| | | |
| | | |
| | | |
| | | |
| | | |

## UTILITIES

| CREDITOR | DUE DATE | MO. PAYMENT |
|----------|----------|-------------|
| | | |
| | | |
| | | |
| | | |

# THE BUDGET
## Know your income and expenses

### INSURANCE

| PROVIDER | DUE DATE | MO. PAYMENT |
| --- | --- | --- |
| _____ | _____ | _____ |
| _____ | _____ | _____ |
| _____ | _____ | _____ |
| _____ | _____ | _____ |
| _____ | _____ | _____ |
| _____ | _____ | _____ |

### SAVINGS / INVESTMENTS

| PROVIDER | DUE DATE | MO. PAYMENT |
| --- | --- | --- |
| _____ | _____ | _____ |
| _____ | _____ | _____ |
| _____ | _____ | _____ |
| _____ | _____ | _____ |
| _____ | _____ | _____ |

# THE BUDGET
*Know your income and expenses*

## Expenses

• •

### MISC. EXPENSES [GYM MEMBERSHIPS ETC.]

| PROVIDER | DUE DATE | MO. PAYMENT |
|----------|----------|-------------|
| _____ | _____ | _____ |
| _____ | _____ | _____ |
| _____ | _____ | _____ |
| _____ | _____ | _____ |
| _____ | _____ | _____ |
| _____ | _____ | _____ |

TOTAL EXPENSES          $_____

# CREDIT CARD TRACKER
## *knowing your limits*

| PROVIDER | DUE DATE | MO. PAYMENT |
|----------|----------|-------------|
| _____ | _____ | _____ |
| _____ | _____ | _____ |
| _____ | _____ | _____ |
| _____ | _____ | _____ |
| _____ | _____ | _____ |
| _____ | _____ | _____ |

TOTAL INCOME      − $_____

TOTAL EXPENSES      $_____

= 

TOTAL EXPENSES      $_____

# THE REVIEW
## How did you do this month?

# Accountability Check!

Did you stick to your goals? Is your budget on track or did you have a moment of weakness?

# THE BUDGET
*Know your income and expenses*

PAYCHECK #1     $_____

PAYCHECK #2     $_____

PAYCHECK#3     $_____

TOTAL     $_____

## Expenses

HOUSING

| CREDITOR | DUE DATE | MO. PAYMENT |
|----------|----------|-------------|
| _____ | _____ | _____ |
| _____ | _____ | _____ |
| _____ | _____ | _____ |
| _____ | _____ | _____ |
| _____ | _____ | _____ |
| _____ | _____ | _____ |

# THE BUDGET
## Know your income and expenses

## LOANS/DEBT

| CREDITOR | DUE DATE | MO. PAYMENT |
|----------|----------|-------------|
| _____ | _____ | _____ |
| _____ | _____ | _____ |
| _____ | _____ | _____ |
| _____ | _____ | _____ |
| _____ | _____ | _____ |
| _____ | _____ | _____ |

## UTILITIES

| CREDITOR | DUE DATE | MO. PAYMENT |
|----------|----------|-------------|
| _____ | _____ | _____ |
| _____ | _____ | _____ |
| _____ | _____ | _____ |
| _____ | _____ | _____ |
| _____ | _____ | _____ |

# THE BUDGET
## Know your income and expenses

Expenses

## INSURANCE

| PROVIDER | DUE DATE | MO. PAYMENT |
|----------|----------|-------------|
| | | |
| | | |
| | | |
| | | |
| | | |

## SAVINGS / INVESTMENTS

| PROVIDER | DUE DATE | MO. PAYMENT |
|----------|----------|-------------|
| | | |
| | | |
| | | |
| | | |
| | | |

# THE BUDGET
*Know your income and expenses*

## Expenses

### MISC. EXPENSES     [GYM MEMBERSHIPS ETC.]

| PROVIDER | DUE DATE | MO. PAYMENT |
|----------|----------|-------------|
| _____ | _____ | _____ |
| _____ | _____ | _____ |
| _____ | _____ | _____ |
| _____ | _____ | _____ |
| _____ | _____ | _____ |
| _____ | _____ | _____ |

TOTAL EXPENSES     $_____

# CREDIT CARD TRACKER
## Knowing your limits

| PROVIDER | DUE DATE | MO. PAYMENT |
|----------|----------|-------------|
| _____ | _____ | _____ |
| _____ | _____ | _____ |
| _____ | _____ | _____ |
| _____ | _____ | _____ |
| _____ | _____ | _____ |
| _____ | _____ | _____ |

| | | |
|---|---|---|
| TOTAL INCOME | − | $_____ |
| TOTAL EXPENSES | | $_____ |
| | = | |
| TOTAL EXPENSES | | $_____ |

# THE REVIEW
## How did you do this month?

---
---

# Money Mantra:

## I deserve

# THE BEST

## and I accept it now

# THE BUDGET
## Know your income and expenses

## Income

PAYCHECK #1          $_____

PAYCHECK #2          $_____

PAYCHECK#3           $_____

TOTAL                $_____

## Expenses

### HOUSING

| CREDITOR | DUE DATE | MO. PAYMENT |
|----------|----------|-------------|
| _____ | _____ | _____ |
| _____ | _____ | _____ |
| _____ | _____ | _____ |
| _____ | _____ | _____ |
| _____ | _____ | _____ |
| _____ | _____ | _____ |

# THE BUDGET
## *Know your income and expenses*

## LOANS/DEBT

| CREDITOR | DUE DATE | MO. PAYMENT |
|----------|----------|-------------|
| _____ | _____ | _____ |
| _____ | _____ | _____ |
| _____ | _____ | _____ |
| _____ | _____ | _____ |
| _____ | _____ | _____ |
| _____ | _____ | _____ |

## UTILITIES

| CREDITOR | DUE DATE | MO. PAYMENT |
|----------|----------|-------------|
| _____ | _____ | _____ |
| _____ | _____ | _____ |
| _____ | _____ | _____ |
| _____ | _____ | _____ |
| _____ | _____ | _____ |

# THE BUDGET
*Know your income and expenses*

## Expenses

### INSURANCE

| PROVIDER | DUE DATE | MO. PAYMENT |
|----------|----------|-------------|
| _____ | _____ | _____ |
| _____ | _____ | _____ |
| _____ | _____ | _____ |
| _____ | _____ | _____ |
| _____ | _____ | _____ |
| _____ | _____ | _____ |

### SAVINGS / INVESTMENTS

| PROVIDER | DUE DATE | MO. PAYMENT |
|----------|----------|-------------|
| _____ | _____ | _____ |
| _____ | _____ | _____ |
| _____ | _____ | _____ |
| _____ | _____ | _____ |
| _____ | _____ | _____ |

# THE BUDGET
## Know your income and expenses

## Expenses

### MISC. EXPENSES  [GYM MEMBERSHIPS ETC.]

| PROVIDER | DUE DATE | MO. PAYMENT |
|----------|----------|-------------|
| _____ | _____ | _____ |
| _____ | _____ | _____ |
| _____ | _____ | _____ |
| _____ | _____ | _____ |
| _____ | _____ | _____ |
| _____ | _____ | _____ |

TOTAL EXPENSES        $_____

# CREDIT CARD TRACKER
*Knowing your limits*

| PROVIDER | DUE DATE | MO. PAYMENT |
|---|---|---|
| _____ | _____ | _____ |
| _____ | _____ | _____ |
| _____ | _____ | _____ |
| _____ | _____ | _____ |
| _____ | _____ | _____ |
| _____ | _____ | _____ |

TOTAL INCOME    - $_____

TOTAL EXPENSES    - $_____

= 

TOTAL EXPENSES    $_____

# THE REVIEW
## How did you do this month?

_____

_____

_____

_____

_____

_____

_____

_____

_____

_____

_____

_____

_____

_____

# Accountability Check!

Did you stick to your goals? Is your budget on track or did you have a moment of weakness?

# THE BUDGET
*Know your income and expenses*

## Income

PAYCHECK #1            $_____

PAYCHECK #2            $_____

PAYCHECK#3             $_____

TOTAL                 $_____

## Expenses

### HOUSING

| CREDITOR | DUE DATE | MO. PAYMENT |
| --- | --- | --- |
| _____ | _____ | _____ |
| _____ | _____ | _____ |
| _____ | _____ | _____ |
| _____ | _____ | _____ |
| _____ | _____ | _____ |
| _____ | _____ | _____ |

# THE BUDGET
*Know your income and expenses*

## Expenses

### LOANS/DEBT

| CREDITOR | DUE DATE | MO. PAYMENT |
|----------|----------|-------------|
| _____ | _____ | _____ |
| _____ | _____ | _____ |
| _____ | _____ | _____ |
| _____ | _____ | _____ |
| _____ | _____ | _____ |
| _____ | _____ | _____ |

### UTILITIES

| CREDITOR | DUE DATE | MO. PAYMENT |
|----------|----------|-------------|
| _____ | _____ | _____ |
| _____ | _____ | _____ |
| _____ | _____ | _____ |
| _____ | _____ | _____ |
| _____ | _____ | _____ |

# THE BUDGET
## Know your income and expenses

## INSURANCE

| PROVIDER | DUE DATE | MO. PAYMENT |
| --- | --- | --- |
| _____ | _____ | _____ |
| _____ | _____ | _____ |
| _____ | _____ | _____ |
| _____ | _____ | _____ |
| _____ | _____ | _____ |
| _____ | _____ | _____ |

## SAVINGS / INVESTMENTS

| PROVIDER | DUE DATE | MO. PAYMENT |
| --- | --- | --- |
| _____ | _____ | _____ |
| _____ | _____ | _____ |
| _____ | _____ | _____ |
| _____ | _____ | _____ |
| _____ | _____ | _____ |

# THE BUDGET
*Know your income and expenses*

## Expenses

### MISC. EXPENSES     [GYM MEMBERSHIPS ETC.]

| PROVIDER | DUE DATE | MO. PAYMENT |
|----------|----------|-------------|
| _____ | _____ | _____ |
| _____ | _____ | _____ |
| _____ | _____ | _____ |
| _____ | _____ | _____ |
| _____ | _____ | _____ |
| _____ | _____ | _____ |

TOTAL EXPENSES     $_____

# CREDIT CARD TRACKER
*Knowing your limits*

| PROVIDER | DUE DATE | MO. PAYMENT |
|----------|----------|-------------|
| _____ | _____ | _____ |
| _____ | _____ | _____ |
| _____ | _____ | _____ |
| _____ | _____ | _____ |
| _____ | _____ | _____ |
| _____ | _____ | _____ |

TOTAL INCOME     − $_____
TOTAL EXPENSES     $_____

= 

TOTAL EXPENSES     $_____

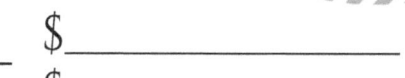

# THE REVIEW
## How did you do this month?

_____

_____

_____

_____

_____

_____

_____

_____

_____

_____

_____

_____

# Money Mantra:

## I am

# ALLOWED

## to be wealthy

# THE BUDGET
*Know your income and expenses*

## Income

PAYCHECK #1     $_____

PAYCHECK #2     $_____

PAYCHECK#3     $_____

TOTAL     $_____

## Expenses

### HOUSING

| CREDITOR | DUE DATE | MO. PAYMENT |
|---|---|---|
| _____ | _____ | _____ |
| _____ | _____ | _____ |
| _____ | _____ | _____ |
| _____ | _____ | _____ |
| _____ | _____ | _____ |
| _____ | _____ | _____ |

# THE BUDGET
*Know your income and expenses*

Expenses

## LOANS/DEBT

| CREDITOR | DUE DATE | MO. PAYMENT |
|---|---|---|
| _____ | _____ | _____ |
| _____ | _____ | _____ |
| _____ | _____ | _____ |
| _____ | _____ | _____ |
| _____ | _____ | _____ |
| _____ | _____ | _____ |

## UTILITIES

| CREDITOR | DUE DATE | MO. PAYMENT |
|---|---|---|
| _____ | _____ | _____ |
| _____ | _____ | _____ |
| _____ | _____ | _____ |
| _____ | _____ | _____ |
| _____ | _____ | _____ |

# THE BUDGET
*Know your income and expenses*

## Expenses

### INSURANCE

| PROVIDER | DUE DATE | MO. PAYMENT |
|----------|----------|-------------|
| _____ | _____ | _____ |
| _____ | _____ | _____ |
| _____ | _____ | _____ |
| _____ | _____ | _____ |
| _____ | _____ | _____ |
| _____ | _____ | _____ |

### SAVINGS / INVESTMENTS

| PROVIDER | DUE DATE | MO. PAYMENT |
|----------|----------|-------------|
| _____ | _____ | _____ |
| _____ | _____ | _____ |
| _____ | _____ | _____ |
| _____ | _____ | _____ |
| _____ | _____ | _____ |

# THE BUDGET
*Know your income and expenses*

## Expenses

### MISC. EXPENSES     [GYM MEMBERSHIPS ETC.]

| PROVIDER | DUE DATE | MO. PAYMENT |
|----------|----------|-------------|
| _____ | _____ | _____ |
| _____ | _____ | _____ |
| _____ | _____ | _____ |
| _____ | _____ | _____ |
| _____ | _____ | _____ |
| _____ | _____ | _____ |

TOTAL EXPENSES     $_____

# CREDIT CARD TRACKER
*Knowing your limits*

| PROVIDER | DUE DATE | MO. PAYMENT |
|----------|----------|-------------|
| _____ | _____ | _____ |
| _____ | _____ | _____ |
| _____ | _____ | _____ |
| _____ | _____ | _____ |
| _____ | _____ | _____ |
| _____ | _____ | _____ |

TOTAL INCOME       − $_____

TOTAL EXPENSES      $_____

= 

TOTAL EXPENSES      $_____

# THE REVIEW
*How did you do this month?*

# Accountability Check!

Did you stick to your goals? Is your budget on track or did you have a moment of weakness?

# THE BUDGET
*Know your income and expenses*

## Income

PAYCHECK #1          $_____
PAYCHECK #2          $_____
PAYCHECK#3           $_____

TOTAL                $_____

## Expenses

### HOUSING

| CREDITOR | DUE DATE | MO. PAYMENT |
|----------|----------|-------------|
| _____ | _____ | _____ |
| _____ | _____ | _____ |
| _____ | _____ | _____ |
| _____ | _____ | _____ |
| _____ | _____ | _____ |
| _____ | _____ | _____ |

# THE BUDGET
## Know your income and expenses

## LOANS/DEBT

| CREDITOR | DUE DATE | MO. PAYMENT |
|---|---|---|
| _____ | _____ | _____ |
| _____ | _____ | _____ |
| _____ | _____ | _____ |
| _____ | _____ | _____ |
| _____ | _____ | _____ |
| _____ | _____ | _____ |

## UTILITIES

| CREDITOR | DUE DATE | MO. PAYMENT |
|---|---|---|
| _____ | _____ | _____ |
| _____ | _____ | _____ |
| _____ | _____ | _____ |
| _____ | _____ | _____ |
| _____ | _____ | _____ |

# THE BUDGET
## Know your income and expenses

## Expenses

### INSURANCE

| PROVIDER | DUE DATE | MO. PAYMENT |
|----------|----------|-------------|
| _____ | _____ | _____ |
| _____ | _____ | _____ |
| _____ | _____ | _____ |
| _____ | _____ | _____ |
| _____ | _____ | _____ |
| _____ | _____ | _____ |

### SAVINGS / INVESTMENTS

| PROVIDER | DUE DATE | MO. PAYMENT |
|----------|----------|-------------|
| _____ | _____ | _____ |
| _____ | _____ | _____ |
| _____ | _____ | _____ |
| _____ | _____ | _____ |
| _____ | _____ | _____ |

# THE BUDGET
## Know your income and expenses

## MISC. EXPENSES    [GYM MEMBERSHIPS ETC.]

| PROVIDER | DUE DATE | MO. PAYMENT |
|----------|----------|-------------|
| _____ | _____ | _____ |
| _____ | _____ | _____ |
| _____ | _____ | _____ |
| _____ | _____ | _____ |
| _____ | _____ | _____ |
| _____ | _____ | _____ |

## TOTAL EXPENSES        $_____

# CREDIT CARD TRACKER
## *Knowing your limits*

| PROVIDER | DUE DATE | MO. PAYMENT |
|----------|----------|-------------|
| _____ | _____ | _____ |
| _____ | _____ | _____ |
| _____ | _____ | _____ |
| _____ | _____ | _____ |
| _____ | _____ | _____ |
| _____ | _____ | _____ |

| TOTAL INCOME | $_____ |
|--------------|----------------|
| − TOTAL EXPENSES | $_____ |
| = | |
| TOTAL EXPENSES | $_____ |

# THE REVIEW
## How did you do this month?

# Money Mantra:

*I am committed to*

# REACHING

*my financial goals*